D1637190

*Le Petomane*

# Le Petomane

## 1857-1945

by
Jean Nohain
and
F. Caradec

Sherbourne Press, Inc.
Los Angeles

# ACKNOWLEDGMENT

*We have to thank the following for their kind help with our researches: Patrice Boussel, Chérel, Gaston Cony, Jacques Garnier, Jean-Léo, Pascal Pia, Georges Sirot, and Jean Weber.*

JEAN NOHAIN AND F. CARADEC

# CHAPTER ONE

## The Thunderous Popularity of Le Petomane in France

Before presenting the star of this story to the reader, it is important to remember the extraordinary, extravagant place which Le Petomane held in Parisian life between 1892 and 1900. "At this time," writes Marcel Pagnol, "Sarah Bernhardt, Rejane, Lucien Guitry dominated the Paris stage along with the splendid Variety company the mere memory of which still makes actors who saw it when they were young feel modest and immature. These were some of the box office receipts of the time: Sarah Bernhardt 8,000 F, Lucien Guitry 6,500 F, Rejane 7,000 F, Variety 6,000 F. There was also a comic artist making himself heard at the Moulin Rouge. He seemed to be alone on the stage and his backside had more to say than his face. He called himself

Le Petomane and in a single Sunday he took 20,000 F at the box office . . ."

Marcel Pagnol could not have known Le Petomane personally. But three of the best known stars of the music hall—Yvette Guilbert, an unforgettable singer; Vincent Scotto, a great popular musician; and Jacques Charles, a celebrated author and historian of the caf'conc'—have each recalled in their own way the sparkling and funny memories they had of their meeting with this peerless artist.

What they wrote shows the standing and importance of the subject of this book and with what authority Le Petomane served the cause of laughter and the music hall.

*Yvette Guilbert* says: "At the Moulin Rouge I heard the most extraordinary outbursts of laughter, the hilarity was at times almost hysterical. This is how it started. One day Zidler was visited by a sad, pale faced man who told him he was a 'phenomenon' and that his gift would become the talk of Paris.

" 'And what is your gift?'

" 'Well, you see, sir,' his visitor explained in all seriousness, 'I have a breathing arsehole . . .'

" 'Oh! yes?' Zidler said in his cold, deadpan way. The other continued as if he were a professor giving instruction.

" 'You see, sir, my anus is of such elasticity that I can open and shut it at will.'

" 'So what?'

" 'So thanks to this providential function I can absorb any quantity of liquid I may be given . . .'

" 'What's that?' said Zidler 'You drink through your backside? What can I offer you?' he went on ceremoniously.

" 'A large basin of water if you will.'

" 'Mineral water?'

" 'No, thank you, ordinary water please.'

"When the basin was brought the man took off his trousers, revealing a hole in his pants at the necessary place. Then seating himself on the basin, which was filled to the brim, he emptied it and refilled it in no time at all.

"Zidler then said that a slight smell of sulphur spread through the room.

" 'I see, so you manufacture Enghien water!'

"The man gave him a little smile.

" 'Ah, that's not all, sir . . . once I've been rinsed out in this way, if I may so put it, I can expel an almost infinite quantity of odourless gas—and that is the basis of my gift—you see, the principle of intoxication . . .'

" 'Just a minute,' Zidler interrupted, 'let's keep it to simple facts. You're telling me you can fart . . .'

" 'If you like to put it that way,' the other conceded, 'but the unique thing about my act is the deep range of sound I can produce.'

" 'You mean you sing through your backside.'

" 'Well . . . yes.'

" 'Right. Go ahead. I'm listening.'

" 'First the tenor . . . one, next the baritone . . . two, now the bass . . . three . . . the light voice . . . four and the vocaliser . . . five.'

"Zidler now completely captivated cried out:

" 'And the one you call the mother-in-law?'

" 'Here she is,' said Le Petomane.

"And on that Zidler engaged him. On the billboards it read:

*Every evening from 8 to 9*

LE PETOMANE

*The only one who pays no author's royalties*

"Zidler put him in the Elephant in the garden. They fell over themselves to hear him and the

10

*Paris—Le Moulin Rouge. "Ah" said Le Petomane,
"what a marvellous fan for my act."*

laughter, shouting, women's shrieking and the whole hysterical din could be heard a hundred yards away from the Moulin Rouge. When Le Petomane saw his public gripped in this way he shouted 'All together, then, one two three . . .' They joined him in chorus and the whole house was convulsed.

"That Sunday Le Petomane's take was a thousand louis."

*A friend of the caf'conc' Jacques-Charles wrote:*
"The Moulin Rouge put on this raging attraction to which all Paris went, announcing LE PETOMANE triumphantly as 'The only artist who pays no author's royalties.'

"He came on dressed in a red coat and black satin breeches—like Kam-Hill—but . . . not to sing: he did imitations of . . . of anyone you like to name.

"I can truthfully say that I have never seen houses laugh, cry, shout and scream as they did when this little man with his William II moustache, crew cut hair and deadpan face pretended to be unaware of his incongruities.

"People were literally writhing about. Women, stuffed in their corsets, were being carried out by nurses which the cunning manager, Oller, had had stationed in the hall, well displayed in their white uniforms. And it was Oller who directed Le Petomane's act—and it certainly was an act.

"In the auditorium a compère playing up the incredulity would climb up on the stage and announce that there was absolutely no trick and that this outstanding artist had nothing concealed . . . in his pants.

"Then the enthusiasm became delirious. It's almost impossible to imagine the noise people made who wanted to shout even louder, the apoplectic faces, the streaming tears . . . they needed a good quarter of an hour to get their breath back."

*Vincent Scotto remembers:* Vincent Scotto, the author of that unforgettable song, "The little Tonkinese" and of all the popular songs of those times, wrote in his *Memories of Paris:*

"The caf' conc' at that time welcomed anything original. You could watch—and this is a little surprising to our present day eyes— cripples, one-eyed, blind and hunchbacks who certainly had talent.

"One day Oller received a visit from a pale elegant man who claimed to be a 'phenomenon' and who wanted to use his natural gift to make himself rich and famous.

"After the audition the 'phenomenon' was engaged.

"This was the famous Le Petomane who drew all Paris to see him. Oller put him in the basement of the Moulin Rouge. People fell over themselves to hear him and there were nothing but cries of joy and laughter during the performance.

"Le Petomane came on in coat, red breeches, white stockings and gloves, patent leather shoes and he finished his act by blowing out a candle.

"Of course the moment came when he had to stop . . . for lack of breath.

"I saw him again some years ago at Marseille, dreaming only of returning to the stage. 'I think if I were to do one or two vocalisations . . .' he told me.

"But the world no longer had a place for the specialty of this artist . . ."

It is usual and legitimate in a book such as this to bring some light to bear on this personality who nearly a hundred years ago had a special place in France, in Paris, in show business, a place apart but a place in the first rank.

Joseph Pujol belongs to History.

# CHAPTER TWO

## Le Petomane's Son Describes
## His Father's Life and Work

*The unedited pages which follow constitute a definitive document on the life and artistic triumphs of Joseph Pujol, Le Petomane. This little masterpiece is the work of Louis Pujol, the eldest living son of Joseph Pujol. It was written without help but with a respect and consideration which in no way excludes complete objectivity.*

*Louis-Baptiste Pujol, the author of this biography, was born at Marseille on the 23rd September, 1891. He became first an apprentice mechanician at Puteaux and then a fitter. But it was not long before he was taken on by his father at the Theatre Pompadour first as a little clown and then as a "feed."*

*Louis-Baptiste Pujol left Paris in 1908 for*

*Marseille to work partly as a café-concert artist (at the Concerts Sauveur at La Barasse) and partly as a fitter.*

*In 1912 he married a Marseillaise, Germain Vergne. One of their four children, Marcel, a champion cyclist, is known locally in Marseille as "the pedalling fifty-year-old."*

## THE ELDEST SON OF LE PETOMANE SPEAKS

### *by Louis Pujol*

This is the life, the career and some stories about Le Petomane of the Moulin Rouge, my father. His name was Joseph Pujol.

As I am not a writer, I am setting down the facts which can be arranged or amplified at will without offending the truth.

I swear on the Bible and on my father's ashes that all I shall say is the truth and nothing but the truth, as I have always heard it from him, and that I have been present at certain of these events since I was growing up during his career.

### *A family of artists*

The father and mother of Le Petomane (that is to say my grandfather and grandmother) were called François Pujol and Rose Demaury. Both were of Catalan origin but came to Marseille when they were very young. François Pujol was an artisan stone mason and sculptor, much valued for his skill and he gave the City of Marseille several of his masterpieces which can be seen today in the Museum of Fine Arts (Palais Longchamp) where the twisted columns are his work.

Francois Pujol and his wife Rose had five children—three boys and two girls. Joseph, the eldest, became Le Petomane.

He was born on the 1st June, 1857, at nine in the evening at his parents' home, 13 rue des Incurables.

### When a baker marries a butcher

Joseph went to school until he was thirteen, then chose to become a baker. He did his apprenticeship and when fully qualified, his father, the stone mason, set him up as a baker on his own account in a little shop, one of several houses which he had built himself, in the Quartier Saint Charles Chuttes-Lavie, on the corner of the street which today bears his name—rue Pujol.

My father married there in 1883. My mother was called Elizabeth Henriette Oliver and had been born in 1863. She was a nice young Marseillaise, daughter of a meat buyer, who worked in the abattoirs. The butcher's shop of her childhood is still there today and can be seen on the Boulevard Amayen.

Two years after they were married they had a daughter, Marie, who was to be the first of ten children, as it turned out one every two years without interruption which my mother gave to the world to the great joy of Le Petomane, my father, who adored children.

But let us go back a little. The phenomenon became apparent soon after my father left school—an extraordinary phenomenon which affected him deeply and as a result transformed his whole life.

Every summer, as did most Marseilles' families, my grandparents and their children went bathing in the sea. The beaches were not then as luxuriously appointed as they are today—just a few wooden huts here and there and piles of stones which did duty as bathing huts. But the good humour, warmth and pleasure were the same as today. And my father, Joseph, like all young people was very partial to such "aquatic pleasures."

Then one day when he was in the sea he had an extraordinary feeling. When putting his head under the water and holding his breath, he felt an icy cold penetrating his stomach, like a sort of colic. He ran ashore and sought out somewhere private to recover. Flabbergasted he saw water pouring out of himself.

Very frightened, little Joseph went home and told his mother "I think I've got a very bad illness." His mother, seeing him so upset, took him to the doctor to reassure him. The doctor happened to be a typical general practitioner. He just laughed and made a joke of it:

*This is the corner of Rue Pujol and Boulevard Aimé Boissy in Marseille. The arrow in the top left corner shows the house in which Le Petomane was born.*

"Why! it's nothing at all . . . but as you're so worried you'd better stop bathing for a while and play ball on the beach."

Neither the doctor, nor Madame Pujol, nor Joseph himself had understood the shattering accident which had just taken place in my father's body and which was to make of him a specimen unique in the history of science— whilst stopping breathing in through his nose and mouth and by putting his head under water, the sea had come in through his anus . . .

Years passed.

My father, who was a strong young man (he was 6 ft. 2 ins.) was doing his military service with the First Regiment of Cuirassiers at Valence. With his bushy black moustache, solid as a wardrobe, always in good humour like a typical Marseillais, he counted neither his friends nor his luck. One day he retold his curious experience in the sea and his fellow soldiers immediately wanted to know if it would happen again. So on a day's leave he went down to the sea for the experiment and to his astonishment the same phenomenon took place. By helping the penetration of the water by contracting his abdomen muscles, he found out he could take in as much water as he wished. And this time he understood that he was . . . just a cuirassier like anyone else.

So for some time to amuse his friends in private he would eject as a waterspout all the water he had taken in through his rectum. Shouting with laughter his comrades ragged him to death.

From time to time my father practised his new exercise with air instead of with water. He would stop breathing through his nose and mouth, take in air through his back passage and at will blow it out again with all sorts of noise—otherwise called "farts"—a veritable fart fantasia—and it was he himself who thought up the name Le Petomane—a title eagerly seized upon by all the soldiers. "This isn't a regiment of cuirassiers," they shouted, "it's the fire brigade . . . or a regiment of artillery."

The word "fart" is somewhat vulgar. But my father had transformed this action into an art since having taken in air that way he used it to make music or, if you prefer it, to modulate sound from the smallest and almost inaudible to the sharpest and most prolonged, simply according to the contraction of his muscles. He could do what he liked with his stomach—and there was no smell.

After returning to civilian life and while still working in the bakery, my father began singing in music halls since he was really an artist. This was before he had the idea of launching himself as Le Petomane. He wrote and performed his own acts all in comic vein—yokel in a smock (before the great Polin) or quick-change singer with a new rig for each song. More often my father varied his numbers by playing the trombone behind the scenes as he was an equally good musician.

Thus for several years my father continued his job as a baker. But a true vocation began to make itself felt in him. He could make so many people laugh, who knew him, in the sea or in the bakery that his friends one day suggested that he make it into an act and try it out in public.

At first Joseph Pujol did not dare approach a music hall agent. He thought it too risky and was afraid of being rejected. But helped by friends and by an impresario who saw the possibilities in the enterprise, he rented some disused premises at the end of the Boulevard Chave in

Marseille, just above the tramway tunnel on line 68 Saint Pierre-de-Neailles. These premises were to become known as Le Petomane's first theatre.

The show was announced by means of posters and handouts and the first performances were fairly coolly received. But after some days, the show had been so well produced—for there was a lot of genius in Le Petomane—that the hall was filled at every performance. There was no further need to advertise. The public did it for him, first in the quartier and then all over Marseille. It was all laughter, cries of joy and amazement. No one had ever seen such a thing before.

Thus successful all his friends urged him to set off for Paris and try to make it in one of the music halls of the capital.

But Joseph Pujol was a cautious man.

"Before Paris," he said, "I'd like to see if what pleases Marseille also goes in other provincial cities. If success smiles on me again then I'll chance my arm in the capital . . . the dream of my life . . . the Moulin Rouge."

His wisdom was approved by all his friends and relatives in Marseille and he was encouraged in his plans.

"That's it, Joe," they said, "a bit more of the provinces first, then Paris will open its arms to you."

My father set off lightheartedly enough. He had a small bag and all the enthusiasm and courage of youth. Afterwards as he often told us "I took the plunge and set off with all confidence—never once looking back."

*Few traces remain today of these first journeys and first performances. We know he performed at Toulon, at Bordeaux—where he was examined by doctors—and at Clerment-Ferrand. Here is an account of his performance at Clerment-Ferrand which appeared in the local newspaper:*

"Le Petomane gave his performance at Clerment-Ferrand in one of those temporary booths erected in the Jaude Square for the principal annual fairs. He presented himself dressed entirely in black, slippers, leg stockings, black silk breeches folded at the knees, embroidered coat.

"At the beginning of the show, facing the audience, he explained that he had the power of breathing in air by the anus, just as we normally breathe in by the mouth. Then by means of this body of air contained in his intestines, he could at will reproduce all sorts of sounds.

"Then turning his back on the public, he announced the kind of noise he was going to make. I remember having heard the mason's round fart, the timid little fart of the young girl, etc. . . .

"The seance ended with an attempt to run through the gamut of sounds. In reality he produced only four notes, the do, mi, sol and do of the octave. I cannot guarantee that each of these notes was tonally true.

"The whole town is talking about it, even in the salons. A lady of high society known for her sharpness of wit was heard to observe that Le Petomane came in with the rain and went out with the wind.

"People laughed, prices have not been put up, and one can be assured that he has a great future. It was a good evening."

After his triumphs in Marseille, his other provincial successes encouraged my father to risk the big throw. Paris! It was 1892.

Thus one morning having arrived in the capital my father turned his determined step in the direction of the Place Blanche. He studied with confidence the huge and reassuring sails of the fabulous Moulin Rouge.

"I suspect," he said smiling to himself, "that these sails are going to start turning for me." And he added the historic remark, afterwards often repeated "The sails of the Moulin Rouge—what a marvellous fan for my number . . ."

He demanded to see the Director without a moment's hesitation sweeping aside with authority any secretary who dared to try and block his path. He strode into Monsieur Zidler's office.

"I am Le Petomane," he said, "and I want an engagement in your establishment."

The director at first seemed surprised but my father's assurance impressed him and he suggested giving him an audition that same day.

"We'll see this very evening how your act goes down with our public. Let's see if it's as funny as you claim it to be."

My father was sure of himself. He had worked up his act very carefully. He would present himself in an elegant costume. Red coat with a red silk collar, breeches in black satin ruched at the knee. Black stockings and Richelieu patent leather pumps, white butterfly tie and white gloves held in the hand.

My father was never tired of telling us that he had bought this magnificent rig out of his own money and was proud of it. Contrary to what has often been said or implied, the Moulin Rouge paid not a penny towards this splendid attire, worthy of a great star.

"My children," our father would tell us often, "I never had stage fright before going on—not even on my opening night at the Moulin Rouge."

The hour struck. When the compère announced "a sensational act never before seen or heard" there was a long silence in the auditorium until the artist appeared. Then as soon as he was on, he explained what he was going to do. But, in order to get them laughing with him, he had prepared a funny little speech which I can remember word for word, having heard it so often.

This is how Le Petomane presented himself with an ease and good humour which worked beautifully on the public.

"Ladies and Gentlemen, I have the honour to present a session of Petomanie. The word Petomanie means someone who can break wind at will but don't let your nose worry you. My parents ruined themselves scenting my rectum."

During the initial silence my father coolly began a series of small farts, naming each one "This one is a little girl, this the mother-in-law, this the bride on her wedding night (very little) and the morning after (very loud), this the mason (dry—no cement) this the dressmaker tearing two yards of calico (this one lasted at least ten seconds and imitated to perfection the sound of material being torn) then a cannon (Gunners stand by your guns! Ready—fire!) the noise of thunder, etc., etc.

Then my father would disappear for a moment behind the scenes to insert the end of a rubber tube, such as are used for enemas. It was about a yard long and he would take the other end in his fingers and in it place a cigarette which he lit. He would then smoke the cigarette as if it were in his mouth the contraction of his muscles causing the cigarette to be drawn in and then the smoke blown out. Finally my father removed the cigarette and blew out the smoke he had taken in. He then placed a little flute with six stops in the end of the tube and played

*One of the high-spots of his act—blowing out a
candle from a distance of one foot.*

one or two little tunes such as "Le Roid Dago-bett" and, of course, "Au claire de la lune." To end the act he removed the flute and then blew out several gas jets in the footlights with some force. Then he invited the audience to sing in chorus with him.

From the beginning of the "audition" mad laughter had come. This soon built up into general applause. The public and especially women fell about laughing. They would cry from laughing. Many fainted and fell down and had to be resuscitated.

"This was all splendid for me," my father said, "the whole of my act went across without a hitch and full steam ahead."

The director enthusiastically offered my father a month's contract renewable. And since his triumph grew all the time, neither side delayed signing a contract which bound them for several years with the right for Le Petomane to play abroad or elsewhere in France.

My father installed his family in a turreted chalet at Saint Maur des Fosses. There we had servants, who became at the same time friends, and in particular a coachman-cum-valet, Pita-lugue, who also acted as my father's manager.

He had a pretty little English carriage, a cab-
riolet drawn by a mare called Aida and when
he drove it himself all dressed up in his best,
with Le Petomane in the driver's seat, he was
recognised and saluted affectionately as an important personage wherever he went:

"That's Le Petomane who went past
then . . . !"

He was the talk of the town. The more he
acted the more he made them laugh.

I should add here that apart from his work on
stage at the Moulin Rouge, my father would
also give private performances to which only
men were admitted. In these he would appear in
a bathing costume of the times with a great
opening cut in the back to prove to disbelievers
that there was no trickery in it. These strata-
gems were necessary to cut short any rumours
there might be and were agreed as necessary
both by my father and the management of the
Moulin Rouge.

These little private sessions began with the
catalogue of farts, continued with the rubber
hose demonstration, the cigarette and the flute
and then the pipe removed, my father would

blow the Retreat. Then to finish it all off, he would lower himself on to a basin containing about two litres of water, pump it into himself by muscular contraction and then expel it clean and under great pressure.

His private audience, interested from the start, proved just as incapable of withholding their laughter as the ordinary public. Then at the end—no admission having been charged— my father would pass round the plate and each spectator would give what he wished.

One evening my father noticed an exceptionally well dressed man in his audience. He was in full formal dress, with frock coat, light bowler hat and a monocle in his eye. When the plate came round he discreetly put in a 20 franc golden piece. My father looked at him and said:

"Thank you, sir, but what change shall I give you?"

The man leant towards him and said in a low voice:

"Keep it all. I am the King of the Belgians."

Leopold II used often to come incognito to Paris, which he loved so much, and felt he simply had to see Le Petomane personally.

"I know you've recently been in Brussels," he whispered smiling, "and you had a great success. My countrymen loved you and laughed a lot. I had to envy them from afar. You must understand that in Brussels my movements are watched and if I had been privately to see Le Petomane . . . at home! So I had to come here secretly to congratulate you."

Brussels, Antwerp, Ghent, Liege—it was in Belgium that Le Petomane began his foreign tours. There as everywhere else he was a raging success.

In Spain, on the other hand, an extraordinary adventure befell him. A sprightly impresario, of the toreador type, came to the Moulin Rouge and signed him up on a magnificent contract for Madrid to play for one month for 40 gold louis per performance (roughly £1,500 today). The journey at that time was endless, expresses being in name only. Le Petomane went alone as he always did. Arriving dead tired, he went straight to the theatre to rehearse his act with the orchestra in the usual way. The director, an impressive moustachioed hidalgo, raised his eyebrows and began to stare down Le Petomane from the very start. At the end of three minutes—scarcely at the point of the wedding night—his fury exploded:

"A foreigner! A Frenchman! A mountebank! And he comes here to insult and outrage the Spaniards! Arrest him! Police, police! Consul! Ambassador! . . . this is a diplomatic incident. It's War! . . ."

Joseph Pujol did not react. In Paris the impresario had seen his act and knew perfectly well that it wasn't just another clacking of castanets . . . the contract had been indubitably signed. With or without his farts Le Petomane had filled his part of the bargain and he was not going to leave without his pesetas.

Arbitration was sought and finally to justify his big contract fee, Joseph Pujol—proving once again that he was both a genius and adaptable artist—replaced his usual act by imitating a clown. So all ended well. The improvised act amused the Spanish and the contract was fully honoured. But the Madrid public never knew that it was the famous Le Petomane who had been announced with such a splurge of publicity.

In addition to Belgium and Spain Joseph Pujol used his weeks of freedom from his Mou-

*In Madrid Le Petomane improvised an act as a clown*
*in order to fulfil his engagement (See page 36)*

lin Rouge contract to visit Algiers (Casino Bab-el-Oued) and Cairo where his success was equally astonishing.

*Arabs and colonists alike remember even today the extraordinary tour Joseph Pujol made through North Africa. They still talk about this journey and his act. In Gaston Bonrepaux's book "Our Blackfooted French Ancestors" (Regain 1965) a long description can be found of Pujol's tour in Algeria which paints an unforgettable picture of the reactions he got from those overseas audiences of the period:*

". . . The cinema had just come to North Africa. On Thursday all the rogues of the town of Bizerta collected together in the one and only hall. The real draw consisted of the ability to throw peanut shells and gourd rind from the gallery (where a seat cost two sous) down on to the orchestra stalls (one franc).

"It must be said, to excuse the Africans, that the phenomenon of Le Petomane had come from France. This rabelaisian personality appeared in Tunis and was adopted by the Bone public even though he was from Toulon.

"He had an unbelievable talent. He had entertained Parisian audiences, doubling them up with laughter. He could produce 'air' at will from the backside and this he used by means of a pipe concealed in his ample breeches and emerging from his coat sleeve.

"This Toulonnais, Le Petomane, had appeared at the Moulin Rouge from 1906 to 1910. He was called Pujol and he had been top of the bill.

"He had triumphed not only with ordinary people but also with the middle classes whom he had writhing about in their boxes and stalls. Society and aristocracy, one knows, would adore to laugh like the common herd but only when in such company, as they say.

"Once on a visit to uncle Berg at the Municipal Casino of Tunis, Cesar Vella was present when the Toulonnais did his extraordinary act, playing wind instruments . . . by manipulating his pelvis.

"Vella was ecstatic.

" 'He does it all without opening his trap. God knows how.' And recounting it all to his friends when he returned to Bizerta.

" 'But he produces air from down below—and plays the ocarina with it. Sole mio! I heard it with my own ears. How does he do it?'

" 'Don't try and pull that one on us,' his mates replied, 'who do you think you're fooling?'

" 'I swear on my grandmother's tomb and I'm a fartass myself if I'm not telling you the truth' said Vella, who had certainly played a part in launching these 'airy' distractions.

"Among Africans it was quite natural to break wind after eating a meal topped with red watermelon, after spiced couscous and garlic macaroons. Thus the prowess of the Toulonnais did the opposite of scandalising them.

"This unexpected noise—especially coming all the way from France—had certainly made the gossips laugh. It was only the Arabs who judged it in bad taste and this provoked a discussion between Mohammed Guerbi and Cesar Vella.

" 'The French are shameless—why they don't think twice about farting—even professionally in the theatre.'

" 'And why not?' Vella retorted, 'if it makes people laugh?'

"And playing it back into the Mussulman's field Vella went on: 'When you eat watermelon and you belch you say "Allah be praised." Le Petomane does it from the other end and doesn't call on the Almighty. I tell you, when I saw this Frenchman farting away professionally and people paying to hear him, I pissed myself laughing. . . .' "

Unfortunately these tours put vagabond ideas into my father's head. And each day his sense of independence grew. He was afraid of being at the mercy of a director and dreamed of becoming his own master. For some considerable time an idea had been haunting him—to own a travelling theatre, "his" theatre.

Several rows had already taken place between him and the management of the Moulin Rouge. My father would certainly have preferred an amicable cancellation of his contract with the Moulin Rouge. But the director refused categorically to discuss it and so on a sudden impulse my father decided to quit and never appeared again at the Elephant, the scene of so many of his triumphs.

As will be seen later on in the legal chapter, the Moulin Rouge began a lawsuit which my

*The garden of the Moulin Rouge with the famous elephant. This was the scene of Le Petomane's first triumph.*

father lost—but this did not stop him going on with his ideas.

So it was about 1895, therefore, soon after leaving the Moulin Rouge that Le Petomane had a charming little touring theatre built some twenty yards long with galleries, paintings and sculptured wood which he called "Theatre Pompadour." In this theatre he was at last going to have things his own way.

"Maybe I'll fart less loudly," he said to his friends, "but I shall be free! Ouf!"

Antoine, the celebrated creator of the Theatre of Liberty was born a year after my father in 1858.

"Just like him," Pujol would say, "I now have Le Petomane's Theatre of Liberty."

The Pompadour Theatre was a real Variety house with a full bill which, of course, Le Petomane topped. But here it must be said that my father was no longer satisfied with usual imitations (young girl, bride, mother-in-law, etc.). He had put his act into verse and added a number in which he imitated animals and birds. The following is the text of "Chanticleer." He wrote the words himself and the music was by G. Chiron, as shown on the manuscript:

44

Old cock of the village—my name's Chanticleer
My plumage is tattered—my voice very clear
Now tonight, my dear public, I'd like to present
Some friends from the barnyard, each one an
    event. *Spoken*
I'd like to start up—with an eight day old pup.
                      *Imitation*
Now dogs of all kinds I can do by the score
We next hear the watchdog—his tail caught in
    the door. *Imitation*
Patau, his old father, wants to help him be freed
But alas and alack, why! he's still on the lead.
                      *Imitation*
The all-seeing blackbird is out of his cage
Mocking and laughing them all into rage.
                      *Imitation*
The blackbird declares that there's clearly a
    plot
To kill Chanticleer—and the owl laughs a lot.
                      *Imitation*
They chatter and chortle, discuss and surmise
Awaiting the Cock who makes the sun rise.
                      *Imitation*
Next comes the duck who is stretching his wings

45

His quack makes you laugh but just wait till he sings. *Imitation*

Here come the bees with a hum and a swish

Waiting their turn to get into the dish.

*Imitation*

Now a hen laying eggs makes a terrible racket

From the sounds that we hear, it's not one—it's a packet. *Imitation*

Chanticleer, in his turn and to prove his devotion,

Warbles away to calm down his emotion.

*Imitation*

Tomcat in his basket wakes up when it's night

And makes love to his lady until it is light.

*Imitation*

Down by the pond at the side of the road

Sits the raucous voiced, ugly, repellent old toad.

*Imitation*

In a neighbouring thicket a nightingale sings

Though we hear him much less as autumn takes wings. *Imitation*

In December it's cold and down comes the snow

Covering the ground like a tomb in one go

The poor and the needy—does anyone care?

Have all lost their homes and are out in the air.

But Christmas Eve comes! Alas! for the beasts

Cruel farmers will slaughter them all for their
  feasts
That well fattened pig—his sad end is nigh
Destiny calls—he'll be part of a pie. *Imitation*
Dear Public, if now that I've given you cause
Reward Chanticleer with your welcome ap-
  plause
If you come back tomorrow, I'll always be
  proud
To keep you amused with my song small and
  loud . . .

In addition to Le Petomane's own act, the bill
at the Pompadour Theatre carried an exhibition of mime. This consisted of groups of three
or five people—my brother Henry, myself, a
professional mime and one or two of the orchestra players (cornet and trombone players) or
the manager Pitalugue.

We wore white tights, cardboard wigs and we
made up our faces white. It looked good and
was very funny. We did turn and turn about
"The Castaway (The Drowned Child)," "The
Prodigal Son," "The Blind and the Paralytic,"
"The Wounded Warrior." The final climax was
composed of a social and pathetic group called
"The Defence of the Home."

47

After the mime, the public were treated to an interesting black magic act given by my elder sister, billed as "The Little Fairy Marzillia."

The principle of this was as follows: my sister Marzillia, the little fairy, would be on stage brightly lit by acetyline and dressed all in white, while Pitalugue, the manager, dressed in black hid in the shadowy part of the stage and handed Marzillia luminous objects which seemed to dance all around her. The effect was captivating and in contrast with the thundering of my father achieved its success by charm.

And so life went on through those years after la Belle Epoque until 1914. The war, alas, brutally broke up Le Petomane's career and destroyed our peace and happiness. Pujol's four

*We used to run to the Theatre Pompadour as soon as we came out of school. Father was always ready for a game with us children.*

sons were mobilised—Henry, Louis, Georges and Francis. One became a prisoner-of-war and two were invalided. After the 1918 armistice, my father was so shattered by his trials and tribulations, that he did not have the heart to take up his artistic career again.

Quietly and without fuss he decided to devote himself to his first job and to his large family. He ran bakeries with his sons and unmarried daughters at first in Marseille until 1922 and then at Toulon where he set up a sizeable biscuit factory which his sons and daughters managed.

With ten children of his own, he now had numerous grandchildren of both sexes and his great pleasure as he grew old was to feel their little arms round his neck and to hear himself called grandad in their little voices.

His wife, our mother Elizabeth Henriette, unfortunately died in 1930.

And so it went on until the war of 1939 and Joseph Pujol never left Toulon again.

Soon after the allied landings in 1945 the great artist died at the age of 88, surrounded by all his children and innumerable friends in tears. He was buried in the cemetery of La

Valette in Var where his tomb can be seen.

Throughout his long busy and happy life, so full of fame and popularity, my father Le Petomane was never once ill. He never called in a doctor and took good care of himself. Every morning after his evacuation he would give himself an enema by the means described earlier using some two litres of warm water and he was thus always meticulously clean.

Unforgettable Joseph Pujol! His public, his friends, his family, all who met and knew him—now, alas, becoming less and less numerous—all remember him as an artist and as an exceptionally gay and simple man who loved to laugh and make others laugh.

In spite of his international success never once did he exhibit any bitterness, jealousy nor unbridled ambition. It could be said that he was always grateful for the gift he had been given by nature and without which he could not have so successfully entertained his contemporaries.

The Faculty of Medicine offered the sum of 25,000 francs for the right to examine his body after his death. My father fully aware of the importance of such a sum of money to all of us was perfectly agreeable to this. But none of us

*The last photograph of a fine gentleman, Joseph Pujol on his 80th birthday.*

would sign an authorisation which would merely have added to our distress in losing a man such as him.

Le Petomane died in untroubled serenity. In the course of his long life, he had given of his best.

## CHAPTER THREE

# Le Petomane's Muscular Control
# Astonishes the French Doctors

The study of the abdomen is as old as medicine itself and the different phenomena produced in the stomach of man have never ceased to intrigue the experts. It is known that one of the most ancient remedies in the world has always been the enema the uses of which Pujol was able to dispense with all his life.

Pliny the younger revealed that the Egyptians had adopted it since the most ancient times. The use of the enema was suggested to them by the ibis and the stork whose long beaks could be inserted in the anus and thereby introduce liquid to cleanse the intestines.

As well as the abdomen, doctors were evidently interested in all contractions of that important part of the body especially in so far as they affected wind about which many contradictory theories were current in the Universities.

One of the most widespread of these was that of the famous School of Salerno in the XIth century. This school was founded in the gulf of Naples by four well-known doctors—a Greek, an Italian, a Jew and an Arab.

At Salerno where the Crusaders came to recuperate the harmful effects of "wind held in" were spoken of freely in the Health Code:

*Quatuor ex vente veniunt in ventre retente,*
*Spamus, hydrops, colica et vertigo, haec res*
  *probat ipsa.*

*To release certain winds is considered almost*
  *a crime.*
*Yet those who suppress them risk dropsy, con-*
  *vulsions,*
*Vertigo and frightful colics.*
*These are too often the unhappy outcome*
*Of a sad discretion.*

Some hundreds of years later, Michel Eyquem de Montaigne advanced the same theory:

"That staunch upholder of will-power Saint

Augustine (*Cite de Dieu* Book XIV, Chapter XXIV) claims to have seen someone in such control of his backside that he could break wind at will and follow the tone of verses spoken to him.

"God alone knows how many times our bellies, by the refusal of one single fart, have brought us to the door of an agonising death. May the Emperor who gave us the freedom to fart where we like, also give us the power to do so."

Michel de Montaigne
*On the Force of Imagination*
Book I, Chapter XXI

Centuries and centuries were still to go by. The works of the Egyptians, Chinese, Greeks, Romans, of the East and of the Arab countries showed no progress in one of the most important areas of human possibility—the effect of will power on the abdominal muscles. Until, at last, Joseph Pujol was himself to take the great step forward.

Pujol opened new horizons to medicine. And as Doctor Adrien Charpy has so aptly written (see later) it is Pujol who, by freely making himself available for innumerable medical observations, fully deserves the title bestowed upon him by the medical profession of Pioneer.

The first reports on "The absorption and expulsion at will of air and liquid by the rectum" are to be found in *Gazette hebdomadaire des Sciences medicales* (Bordeaux 20 March, 1892) and in the *Journal de Medecine* of Bordeaux (27 March, 1892).

However it is Doctor Marcel Baudouin to whom we owe the most complete and definitive scientific study. This appeared in 1892 in *La Semaine Medicale*. It is the complete answer today to any detailed question which can be put and to the scepticism, in particular, of certain detractors of France's great citizen, Le Petomane.

## An Extraordinary Case of Rectal Breathing and of Musical Anus

### by Dr. Marcel Baudouin

Every evening at the Moulin Rouge, a young man has for some time conducted in a private room a series of purely physiological exercises, which by reason of their somewhat special character excite an extreme degree of curiosity, astonishment and incredulity amongst the public frequenting this establishment.

We attended several of the public sessions in the course of which the subject only performs a part of what he can do. We have also had the good fortune to be able to examine at leisure—and in the best conditions—different exercises. One of the most important was in the laboratory of Monsieur Poirier at the Practical School of the Faculty of Medicine. This examination was under the direction of Charles Richet, Professor of Physiology, and of Doctor Poirier, the duly appointed Professor in charge of Anatomy.

Under these conditions it was easy to ensure that there was nothing supernatural or artificial. There is no doubt that this man is of perfect good faith and that he simply puts to use unprecedented but physiologically explicable phenomena which are real and rely on no trickery whatever. They are also of the very greatest scientific interest. We therefore thought it of interest to publish our detailed observation of this curious matter.

We are also indebted to Doctors Richet and

Poirier for their valuable help and advice in what follows.

The subject in question, Le Petomane, is a vigorous solid man of 35 years, intelligent, married and the father of four children. He is tall (over 6 ft.) and has a physique in which nothing is exaggerated, except for certain muscles—those which he exercises most frequently in his somewhat unusual profession—and is in first rate condition. He has never been ill and has no hernia. He has no malformation. There were no varicose veins in his interior members and his vein system had no modification.

In a state of repose the anus shows no sign of abnormality but is perhaps a little more dilated than is usual. The sphincter is strong and elastic. There are no haemorroids in spite of the muscular work which takes place in this region every day, as we shall see. The rectum too is normal and does not seem dilated.

Even before the age of thirteen, he had become aware of a special ability he had for expelling through his anus—without knowing how—any gas accumulated in his digestive tube producing, in the process, noises of a greater or lesser intensity. His young friends were immediately struck by his genuine superiority in this kind of exercise and to cash in on this our bright young man wished to do even better. So he did exercises and developed an extraordinary ability, without quite knowing how.

Soon he began to tour the towns of the Midi exploiting his speciality at Cette, Beziers, Nimes, Toulouse, etc. Recently he was in Bordeaux where he was examined, so he told us, by several professors of the Faculty of Medicine. He was presented to the Society of Anatomy and Physiology in that city by Monsieur Petit and was examined at the Hospital Saint-André. This is the first time he has been in Paris.

Le Petomane carries out two sorts of exercises, different in appearance, but in reality identical, the substratum only being different.

1. The first which are done in public because he cannot make use of natural facilities, for obvious reasons, consist exclusively in taking in air by the anus into the large intestine, and perhaps even into the small intestine, in quantity and then in expelling this air imprisoned in the last part of the digestive tube under given

conditions. This process results in the production of sounds of differing tonality and intensity according to the circumstances.

This phenomenon may be considered similar to the example given by Professor Verneuil of the man with the musical anus, a somewhat frivolous description but one which nevertheless clearly describes what takes place when gas enclosed in the intestine is expelled at will.

2. The other exercises are only those of the laboratory, amphitheatre and hospital, if one may so describe them. They cannot be given in public, though they are arranged without difficulty for private viewing. Nevertheless these are the most interesting and to a certain extent are the key to the above noises, which the public at large hears but the reason and cause of which it cannot understand, nor above all realise their scientific implications.

This, as briefly as possible, is what takes place:

1. After the usual introductory speech, Le Petomane, who is standing leans well forward, bending his body so that his thorax is almost horizontal, that is to say perpendicular to his lower members.

(a) Then he grips with his hands the top part of his knees on both sides thus giving a solid support to his upper body. The head is in the direction of the thorax but a little inclined to the ground. He then takes a very little breath and stiffens his arms. He makes certain movements imperceptible to anyone watching who has not been forewarned and his face becomes very congested as well as his neck. There are obvious signs of real and intense strain, which are very easy to observe if the subject is undressed and the exhibition is not taking place in public.

After a few moments and following muscular efforts which are difficult to analyse, the digestive tube is completely filled with as much air as it can contain under such conditions. The subject then gently stands up almost vertical. The reservoir is full and can so remain for a certain time but not for long. Little by little it empties itself of its own accord unnoticed if Le Petomane does not force the air out himself.

(b) The amusing part of this exercise constitutes the second part of the phenomenon—the forcing out of the air accumulated in the intestine, acting as a reservoir, the breathing out.

By expelling this air, either standing upright, leaning forward, or bent double, and by a thousand different ways dependent on the state of contraction or relaxation of the anal sphincter on the one hand and of the muscles controlling the variation in capacity of the abdominal cavity on the other, Le Petomane can obtain effects which are both as brilliant as they are surprising and unforeseen.

When the gas comes out with enough force and with a certain degree of tension from the sphincter, noises are produced of intensity, timbre and of great variety. At times these are genuinely musical sounds. Although as it is almost impossible to obtain given notes these turn out to be common chords or, what is more extraordinary, recognisable tunes.

Le Petomane imitates all sorts of sounds such as the violin, the bass and the trombone. He can produce a strong enough note ten or twelve times running and he can take in enough air to produce sound lasting ten or fifteen seconds.

Without clothes the subject can extinguish a candle at a distance of 12 inches by the force of gas violently expelled from the anus. As this is air which has only been a few moments in the intestine there is no smell such as there would be from gases of intestinal origin.

To sum up these exercises, the intestine plays the rôle of the chest in storing air and the anal sphincter that of the vocal chords, the throat and the mouth.

2. The other exercise which was much more interesting from the physiological point of view—since it was the clearest demonstration possible of willing the aspiration of air by the anus—is as follows:

(a) Le Petomane completely naked plunges his bottom into a big container of water on the ground. In this last case he squats above the container and grips his knees with his hands, as previously described. His upper body is thus firmly immobilised. The same phenomena are then produced: the sharp effort of a particular kind and method of aspiration by means of the dilation of the abdominal cavity.

Water penetrates the large intestine by the anus in small quantities following a series of accumulated efforts. The water in the basin goes down. If by chance the anus is not completely immersed when Le Petomane breathes in, then air enters with the water and produces a characteristic glou-glou comparable to the noise made when we drink too hot a liquid and which ceases when immersion is complete.

When the subject has filled his large intestine right up, he stands up and can retain the water taken in for a certain time.

(b) A curious fact, which demonstrates the power of expulsion of his intestine, thanks to the contraction of the abdominal muscles, is the violence with which he can project the water he has stored. Using all his strength and leaning forward, he can project most of the water he has taken in to a distance of four to five yards in one jet.

When we detailed these facts to Professor Verneuil he showed a lively interest and decided to examine Le Petomane himself at the hospital, asking us to announce this for Thursday, 21st April at 9.30 when Members of the Congress of Surgery would be visiting him to see his work.

After this excellent scientific study where nothing seems to have been left in the dark, few doctors since 1892 have been tempted to add personal developments or remarks to this report.

However in 1904 some pertinent observations

appeared at Toulouse under the signature of Dr. Adrien Charpy, to which we alluded before, entitled: "On the action of will power upon the abdominal muscles."

"The muscles of the anterior abdominal wall can be directed to certain movements. This is in subjects who contract at will and in depth only the large muscles (oblique and transverse) either the right muscles or a part of them; their bellies react in the opposite direction to the regions which tense or relax. This can be seen in Proteus man and in Strangfort.

"This same wall plays an important rôle in Le Petomane's exercises, several cases of which have recently been studied.

"Le Petomane uses his abdominal cavity like a bellows, the anterior and posterior walls being the two valves, the rectum the pipe. He inspires and expires. Crouched in a position which makes breathing difficult, he forces the anterior wall of the stomach against the posterior wall, and as he takes up this first position, a void is caused in the large intestine, air or water fills this through the open anus and the bellows are charged.

"In reverse the muscular wall presses down on

the full colon and causes it to expel air or water to a great distance. By controlling this abdominal pressure, by the clever play of the sphincter and anal relevator, the artist obtains by means of this second mouth some sophisticated effects—he imitates musical instruments, hums recognisable tunes.

"It should be noted that all this was discovered accidentally, whilst bathing, and that this ability has been developed from a natural aptitude by voluntary and continuous work. Hypertrophy of the muscles of the abdominal wall has been noted in the subject most observed and who, moreover, was the pioneer."

Dr. Adrien Charpy, Toulouse, Marques, 1904
*On the Action of the Will on Muscles*

## CHAPTER FOUR

## *Le Petomane's Freedom to*
## *Exercise His Art Curtailed by Law*

In love with independence, enjoying the pleasures of life, wanting only to laugh and make others laugh, Le Petomane was to find himself, between 1894 and 1898, sadly involved in a shattering train of legal events.

The highly unusual profession which Joseph Pujol had been able to adopt, thanks to his exceptional gifts, seemed to him basically and by definition, free of all restraints, rules and regulations.

Without comparing him to "L'Enfant de Boheme" of the song, who would have thought that one day la Petomanie would come to know the laws, law courts, bewigged Judges, Barristers, Recorders and Bailiffs and that Le Petomane called meanwhile to a completely different vocation would become through four years a regular though involuntary star of the Court of Lost Causes!

The business began in 1892 at the height of Joseph Pujol's success at the Moulin Rouge. The Faculty of Medicine was also taking a deep interest in this star who was so simple, so sympathetic, so co-operative and so useful to Science.

Indeed far from having his head turned by the flattery, applause, honours and royal hand-shaking to which he was subjected, Joseph Pujol continued to seek the company of the humble friends of his youth and in particular one of them who kept a Gingerbread stall in the market.

One Sunday evening, after several triumphant but exhausting performances, Joseph Pujol was summoned to the office of Monsieur Oller who managed not only the Moulin Rouge but also another important establishment, the Olympia.

Responsibility for these Pleasure Domes did not exactly make Monsieur Oller into a joker. Dark eyed and gloomy in appearance, he attacked in the most scathing way the worthy

Pujol, who had scarcely had time to remove his rubber tube.

"Is it true," he said, "that you performed your act this afternoon at a gingerbread stall in the market?"

Momentarily thrown Joseph Pujol quickly recovered and made a joke of it as usual:

"My dear sir, forgive me but you astound me!"

He went on to explain gently and with good humour that he had given a very brief run through of one of his simplest and funniest acts to attract buyers to his friend's gingerbread stall —since the autograph craze had not yet come in—but that this was simply a friendly gesture which could in no way damage the professional work he did every evening for the ladies and gentlemen who honoured the Elephant of the Moulin Rouge with their presence.

"And if I were to serve you with a writ?"

Le Petomane coloured up, "You want to bring the Law into this? Go ahead!"

But Oller was beside himself with fury, "I'll cut you down to size," he threatened.

Le Petomane drew himself up to his full

69

height, "You do that," he said, "and I'll simply cut off the gas!"

Doors slammed. It was War!

Joseph Pujol who had for a long time been irritated by his employer's exigencies which continually increased his hours of work, conceived the idea of exercising his talents on his own account.

His friend, the gingerbread lady, had encouraged him in this idea by continually commenting, in a vulgar expression of the time, that with people such as Monsieur Oller there was no point in bursting yourself, they could stuff it . . .

Joseph Pujol did not particularly approve of this crudity, but he wound up by taking the advice of several sharp fairground operators who urged him to set up on his own and be his own director.

The Pompadour Theatre was about to be born.

Le Petomane went on working at the Moulin Rouge for several months longer, but his heart was not in it.

Blind with fury Oller never knew in the morning whether Le Petomane would be there in the evening. Following his whim Joseph Pujol would either say he felt on form or with great regret that his belly would not oblige.

On a certain Saturday night Louis Pujol was the only one to know that the show his father would give that night would be his farewell performance at the Moulin Rouge. Whilst doing his act with a gravity and private emotion—and perhaps with more than usual brilliance—Le Petomane knew he would never again act in front of the Elephant's rustling luxurious drapes to that delirious audience of pleasure seekers and pretty women to whom he owed his fame and reputation.

The next day, Sunday, at the Foire du Thrône the Pompadour Theatre opened its doors.

At the first performance two men in black sat in the front row taking notes. Far from laughing like the rest these visitors, notebook and pencil in hand, took down each phase of the number, every word spoken by Pujol, each and every reaction of the delighted audience. These gentlemen were the Bailiff and his Clerk who were preparing their case.

It was Writ time for Le Petomane.

The summons was issued for the 1st May, 1894, in the 6th Court of the Civil Tribunal of the Seine and the papers of the day made it front page news:

## Le Petomane Sued

"A case certain to make a considerable noise is to be heard in the 6th Court of Civil Tribunal of the Seine, presided over by M. Toutés.

"This is a claim for damages taken out by M. Oller, Manager of the Moulin Rouge and the Olympia, against one of his artists M. Pujol, better known as Le Petomane.

"M. Oller accuses his employee of having violated his terms of employment by giving performances at a gingerbread stall in the market.

"M. Oller is in consequence claiming the payment of a fine by Le Petomane as stated in the contract in the sum of 3,000 francs.

*Le Petit Parisien,* 1st May, 1894"

In the *Petit Journal* of the same date and in spite of the gravity of the case, the Editor saw fit to be facetious and in dubious taste. Unfortunately there are certain members of the Press who respect nothing.

"A resounding case is due to be called today before the 6th Court of the Civil Tribunal of the Seine. M. Oller, manager of the Moulin Rouge, is claiming the sum of 3,000 francs for violation of contract from M. Pujol whose act is entitled 'Le Petomane Fin-de-siecle musician.'

"M. Joseph Pujol is a more or less lyrical artist whose melodies, songs without words, do not come exactly from the heart. To do him justice it must be said that he has pioneered something entirely his own, warbling from the depths of his pants those trills which others, their eyes towards heaven, beam at the ceiling.

"The beak-nosed Monsieur Oller scored a success with this innovator right from the start. He monopolised him. And for many long months the public has flocked to the Moulin Rouge wide eyed and gaping mouthed to applaud with frenzy approaching delirium this artistic offering of the fin-de-siecle.

"All was going well. M. Oller and his employee were living if not in sweet intimacy at least on a basis of peace. Then suddenly this devil of a Le Petomane had the idea of messing it all up by going to a gingerbread stall in the market, without considering his contract, and performing in a tumbledown hut open to the four winds.

"When the Director of the Moulin Rouge heard of this escapade, he had the idea of going after him and bringing him back with some well placed kicks in . . . his musical area; but on reflection and not wishing to damage the instrument he has preferred the law to stick its nose into this affair and is claiming the 3,000 francs fine, stipulated in the agreement.

*Le Petit Journal,* 1st May, 1894"

Both sides pleaded furiously in the case.

The Moulin Rouge claimed that it had largely contributed to the launching of Le Petomane who had become one of the most popular stars with the French public and with foreigners always avid for Parisian curiosities. Joseph Pujol could not legitimately claim a lack of wind or physical deficiency as a reason for going since the very day after leaving the Moulin Rouge he was doing exactly the same act on the stage of a travelling theatre.

74

The lawyer for Joseph Pujol eloquently drew attention to the months of work, strain and professionalism of an artist unsparing of time or trouble. Disheartened by ingratitude and by the growing sordidness of the demands made on him by the management, it was true that Joseph Pujol would often go down to the markets seeking out his old friends and providing a little entertainment to a public which, alas, did not have the means to pay the costly entrance fee to the Moulin Rouge. It was solely because this greedy management had refused any reasonable transaction that Le Petomane had been forced to decide on setting up his own theatre where, responsible only to himself, he could pursue his crusade to make people laugh under popular conditions.

In spite of the ardent pleading of the defence, Joseph Pujol was sentenced to pay 3,000 francs in damages or some £500 at the present day value of money.

La Petomanie and the law had officially brushed together.

Joseph Pujol was put out of countenance by this first experience of the law.

So that is how lawyers, he thought to himself,

can force a free man to make noises with his belly in certain places and circumstances—and only in those places and circumstances under threat of fine and damages . . .

It was not long before he had his revenge and neatly rounded off his differences with the men of law.

Some weeks after his departure from the Moulin Rouge, Joseph Pujol learnt with amazement that the establishment had just engaged and billed—with considerable publicity—a woman Petomane.

His blood boiled. Some other creature was going to deck herself out in the title he had invented himself in his youth and perform publicly in the very same place where he had conquered Paris and won his international notoriety.

Then who was this woman Petomane?

A quick enquiry established that she was nothing but an infamous imposter. In their haste both for revenge and to satisfy the gogglers who demanded their petomanie as usual, the producers of the spectacle had engaged a false woman Petomane, Angele Thiebeau, who worked with a pair of bellows hidden under her skirt. Disgraceful!

Joseph Pujol went back to his lawyer and instructed him to sue for counterfeit and fraudulent imitation.

The lawyer got to work and being a witty man began his attack with a well-known passage from Beroalde de Verville on the trickery—even then—of a courtesan of the sixteenth century who might have been the lineal ancestor of the woman Petomane of the Moulin Rouge.

"Beroalde de Verville in the 'Way of Succeeding' recounts the following: 'The Lord of Lierne, a French gentleman, went to bed with a courtesan in Rome. As chaste courtesans well know their business, she had procured some little pellicules which had been filled with scented air through the skill of perfumers. Having a supply of these wares and holding the gentleman in her arms, the good Imperia allowed herself to be loved. To add an edge to the fondling and to draw her lover more closely, the lady took one of the pellicules in her hand and burst it, thus making the audible sound of a fart. On hearing this the gentleman withdrew his head from the bed to give himself air. "It's not what you think," she said, "you must hear before being afraid." Thus persuaded he received an agreeable odour quite contrary to what he had expected and which he savoured with pleasure. This having been repeated a number of times, he enquired of the lady if such winds proceeded from her considering that they smelt so good and given the fact that similar winds emanating from the lower portions of French ladies were stinking and abominable. To this she replied with a little frisky philosophy to the effect that Italian ladies, due to the nature of the country and the aromatic food and to the use of odoriferous articles produced their quintessence in the lower regions as if it were the neck of a retort. "In truth," he replied, "our own ladies fart in a quite different way."

" 'It so happened that after some more musketry and on account of witholding her wind for too long, Imperia farted naturally, substantially and at length. The Frenchman diligently stuck his nose under the sheets in order to apprehend the good odour which he wished to savour to the full. But he was deceived; he received through his nose a stench of barnyard proportions "Oh!

my dear lady," he said, "what have you done?"
She answered "My lord, I was but paying you a
compliment to remind you of your own country." ' "

By a curious coincidence lawsuits about peto-
manes seemed suddenly to be in fashion. Indeed
even before Joseph Pujol had launched his attack on her, Angele Thiebeau, the phony farter
(as perhaps she might be called today) had herself sued the paper *L'Art Lyrique et le Music
Hall* claiming that it had libelled her in her
profession.

It was not until 1898 that the case was called
after many delays before the 9th Court of the
Correctional Tribunal of the Seine, presided
over by M. Richard. The judgment was savage:

"Mademoiselle Angele Thiebeau is claiming
the payment of 2,000 francs in damages from
the newspaper *L'Art Lyrique et le Music Hall*
by reason of an article published on the plain-
tiff's performances given at the Moulin Rouge.

"The Tribunal having heard the pleading of
Maitre Lagasse for Mlle Thiebeau and of Maitre Coulen for *L'Art Lyrique* renders the following judgment:

"Whereas the woman Thiebeau, called la

79

femme-petomane, is claiming that the defenders have damaged and libelled her in an article in the 13th March, 1898, edition of the paper *L'Art Lyrique et le Music Hall* in which she cites the following passage: 'I am astonished that the management charges one franc to go to the first floor and watch la femme petomane. Without even the excuse of being pretty, she imitates the music in question by means of bellows concealed in her pocket. This is simply a practical joke in bad taste, which the management should never have put on.'

"Whereas the defamation being the imputation to a fact of nature of infringing honour and reputation, the allegation that the prosecution makes use of a trick to ensnare the public and that whilst claiming that she does naturally what in fact is achieved by means of a gadget, can prejudice her pecuniary interests but does not touch her honour or reputation since it is observed that the majority of physical feats produced in public places owe their effectiveness not only to the skill of their authors but also to apparatus and to tricks designed for illusion.

"Whereas it would not be a case of professional reputation being applied to the exploitation of an abnormal physical disposition, alien to the valuation of a personal art or talent.

"Whereas in addition the incriminating article does not personally attack Mademoiselle Thiebeau, the expression 'practical joke in bad taste' not being invective applied to her but the means employed, according to the defence, of misleading the public so this qualification in the same way as the imputation itself cannot be considered a libel.

"Now be it judged that the defence is upheld and the case dismissed."

The false petomane was finished.

Joseph Pujol, without even having had to plead himself, felt completely vindicated. Thus quite simply he withdrew his own lawsuit.

Justice had been done.

# CHAPTER FIVE

## *Le Petomane and French Literature*

Like the frog in the fable, Joseph Pujol huffed
and puffed and "worked on himself" to be able
to do his act. But the frog, whose fate was so
troublesome, only inspired a simple fairy tale of
fourteen verses. Le Petomane's career was to
give birth to a whole varied literature in which
poets and pamphleteers, flattering praise and
denigrating insults were all muddled up. How
could it be otherwise? Did not the author of
"The Frog who wished to become an Ox"—La
Fontaine himself—warn the good Joseph Pujol:
"Critics are a hard lot"? Le Petomane, like
Homer, had his snarling critics. He consoled
himself with the thought that no genius can
escape the jealousy of the impotent censors of
the times.

He had resigned himself to hearing every day as he walked about allusions in bad taste and dirty jokes:

Money doesn't smell . . .

Gone with the wind . . .

One fart chasing another . . .

The French P is a Russian R-se . . .

Suggestive talk merely made Pujol shrug his shoulders and go back more willingly to the work which was his consolation and the meaning of his life.

At the Black Cat, next door to the Moulin Rouge, Maurice Donnay loved the skill and simplicity of Joseph Pujol. "A good workman from the bottom up" he would say of him. "He deserves far more than the sarcasm he gets in certain literary circles." A selection follows of some of the choicer bits, inspired by the hero of this book.

## Le Petomane

Here is a very modern, fin-de-siecle fellow who has found his natural vocation. In spite of frequent failure, he refused to take No for an answer. He went doggedly on insisting that he had a brain and that that was where his talent lay. Soon his conviction began to gain him support. Perhaps he was right after all. Moreover he worked morning, noon and night, filling the house with the sound of his studies.

The most difficult thing was to get himself known. Presenting himself at the offices of one of the big Paris newspapers, he gave an audition—and there he was launched! Another difficulty was to settle upon a suitable title for himself. Was he to call himself le peteur (the farter)? Open the dictionary and what do you read? "Peteur (Farter), someone who has the habit of farting." Should he call himself le peteux? "Insulting expression—to go like a peteux (coward), to leave without dignity (Academie)." It would have to be something else. Then he had an inspiration of genius; he would call himself Le Petomane. The new title would offend no susceptibilities and could be announced in any drawing room. Words have their own dignity.

A huge crowd, eager to hear him, pressed into the theatre—the "tout-Paris" of first nights was there in force. The newcomer stepped down to the front of the stage, and faced the audience, sweat pouring from his brow. He began with a few modest sounds, then more courageously he let himself go. Note followed note as if in a fanfare. The ice was broken, the public applauded vociferously—he was famous. They fight to get to him. Le Petomane is at ease in any milieu. After a monologue gabbled by an actor from the Comedy Francaise, he takes the stage. The mood changes. He ups with his skirts . . . and goes to it . . . noisily. With plenty of tact he knows exactly the right note to strike, discreet in society, matey with the bourgeoisie, serious with politicians and with the common herd he goes flat out, even does it to excess. He knows his public.

Le Petomane is a serious well-balanced man. Ask him about politics and he will answer "Those who listen to only one bell, hear only one sound." If you press him for his opinion he replies simply "I know where the wind comes from"—a thought which might well be pondered by men in public positions.

He has plenty of wit. One evening dining with a great lady he was invited to exhibit his talent after the dessert. Turning to a Captain of Artillery on his right, he made this celebrated retort "When this gentleman has fired his cannon, I will speak."

He tours in the provinces and is everywhere acclaimed, covered with flowers. His talent really gets the old girls. At Soissons he is always offered a ceremonial dish of beans. He enjoys being a celebrity—an industrialist has even marketed an irrigator bearing his name.

Le Petomane does admit to one disappointment. Until now he has not been permitted to take part in religious ceremonies, the priests maintain that his art is too profane. At one time the Church refused burial to actors—who knows what the next relaxation of the rules will be? One of these days perhaps at a friend's wedding, Le Petomane will be able to blow a few moving notes.

Old age, too, brings its sadnesses. As with all

artists age brings a diminishing of the faculties. One evening he will appear on stage but not on form. The pitiless public will whistle where once it shrieked. Le Petomane knows he is finished. He will retire—with death in his soul. Each day he weakens. Occasionally to please a friend he may consent to do his act once more but it won't be the same—he will hardly be able to get out more than a note or two.

Then one fine day he will snuff out and expire with a last . . . sigh.

Eugene Fourrier in
*Gil Blas Illustré* No. 39, 25th September, 1892

## Twenty Days of Pleasure in the Capital

### An Evening at the Moulin Rouge

At the next table to theirs everyone was talking about the absence of Le Petomane who had excused himself to the management, saying that a cold deprived him of his means of working, and Berlurette explained in detail to her companion the whole gamut of the performance given by the famous "nightingale" of the Moulin Rouge. Young Dubassin seized this opportunity of getting back into her good graces.

"Why, there's nothing to that," he said in a loud voice as she continued singing Le Peto-mane's praises, "That trick? I bet anything you like I can sing just as well as he can."

"Done" said a neighbour.

Accepting the challenge Dubassin jumped up

E. GRENET-DANCOURT

# Le
# Ventomane

MONOLOGUE COMIQUE

SOUPIRÉ PAR

## X...

Sociétaire de la Comédie-Française.

**Prix : UN FRANC**

PARIS

PAUL OLLENDORFF, ÉDITEUR

28 *bis*, RUE DE RICHELIEU, 28 *bis*

1893

The title-page from one of the most popular of the satirical tilts at Le Petomane's
performance.

on the table and, in front of a crowd which soon gathered round, adopted Le Petomane's professional stance and began giving the first few notes! This time Berlurette was not embarrassed by her gigolo and that charming waltz "Go, little boy, go where the wind blows you" had never been so happily played.

Philoctete was in good voice. Deep notes and high all came tumbling out sweet and sonorously from his wind instrument. In the chorus of praise which followed there was only one dissident voice from the neighbour furious at losing his bet.

"Yes, yes, not bad but Le Petomane's chest notes are more accentuated than yours."

Feuilleton of Emile Blain
*Paris qui rit,* 6th November, 1892

## E. Grenet-Dancourt

### *Le Ventomane*

Comic monologue by X . . . member of the Comedie-Francaise

Ollendorff, 1893

All my life I shall never forget the first time I saw him or the second time I heard him . . .

astonishing . . . marvellous . . . sublime! Never had I been carried so high into the ether of art . . . never, never, never . . . the moment he came on a great silence descended . . . looking round with a sweet melancholy—almost as if dreaming—he took in the house—and what an audience he had! The nobility from the two Faubourgs and every single literary, artistic and fashionable personality there might be in Paris. . . . (Seriously) Quality will always draw a crowd and even the most blasé display at times a determination to immerse themselves once more in the ideal and to breathe another air than that of every day . . . the Master thus welcomed bowed slightly, put his hands on his knees and with the nonchalance of a lord, smilingly opened his—er—hum! . . . and began. A thrill of excitement ran through the auditorium. To begin with a sweet song like that of a swallow . . . something gentle, timid and tender like the sigh of a young girl . . . of a young girl who has known unhappiness . . . a breath, a mere nothing. . . . Then all of a sudden the note changes and grows—the poem becomes epic . . . hesitant and weak at the start, the voice grows firmer and stronger . . . no longer does it caress, it threatens! Impetuously it growls, thunders, explodes, groans—cyclone—hurricane—tempest! Lightning strikes in the tortured firmament and whilst in the distance a warning gun is fired, distractedly under our very eyes the thunder growls to excess . . . it was terrifying . . . never have I seen such a storm . . . a dry storm, of course, but then they are the worst . . . but hist! . . . listen . . . calm has returned and the gentle song of rocking waves mounts once more in the air . . . oh! harmony . . . harmony . . . harmony!!! And so it went on for two hours . . . we were all of us there hanging on the Master's lips, feverish, gasping—and while the men sought to hide their emotion by biting their moustaches—beneath the velvets, silks and lace the women's breasts heaved tumultuously . . . as for me, I was crying no longer having just enough strength left to applaud the man who was making my tears flow . . . at last he stood up and looking down once more on the audience with his sweet dreaming melancholy, took his farewell and disappeared . . . I went home, my head on fire, and before going to sleep tried myself to reproduce what I had just heard . . . nothing, nothing, nothing. . . . The next morning I began again—the same result . . . indeed even after fifteen days, I was not a step further on . . . not a thing . . . others in my place would have been equally discouraged . . . it's simply not fair . . . when one has a fixed idea and above all when one feels one has something in the wind . . . one fine morning, taking my courage in both hands, I sought out the Master and asked him to instruct me in his method, to give me lessons . . . it's a difficult career, he told me straight away, it's rough going . . . not too much competition till now, young man, but the going is tough . . . and he listed the vexations and difficulties . . . he had himself started very young, very young indeed and it had only been by hard work, perseverance and will power that he had succeeded in making a name for himself and an enviable situation . . . he saw that I had the physical means to hand but that was not enough . . . other qualities were necessary, nay indispensable . . . finally he pointed out that parents often have preconceived ideas and that perhaps my family intended me for some other profession than that of artist. Nevertheless five minutes later he was giving me my first lesson . . . oh! how difficult it is to start . . . I had no voice . . . I was lacking in voice . . . feeling—

yes—plenty of that, gesture and warmth but no vocal ability . . . I was in the pit of despair . . . but he restored my battered courage . . . what's the good of getting angry? he said . . . have patience . . . it will come . . . and it's true, it did . . . after six months of work, twelve hours a day, the voice is there . . . still a little thin in volume . . . but of quality . . . so I am no longer an amateur . . . and what does it matter if the sharps and flats still bother me a little? I'm not doing badly . . . I've already tried it out in one or two drawing rooms—among friends of course . . . and it's been a success . . . a nice little success . . . well, mothers with marriage-able daughters have started giving me the eye . . . and even my parents—well, they're actually proud of me these days . . . so let's get on with it, shall we? I'll give you a little sample of what I can do . . . you'd like it? I have a bit of a cold so you must be indulgent. . . . Right! . . . Hm! . . . It's a question of not being taken short . . . (after a pause) I've got it (bowing graciously at the audience). By the side of a lake, one summer evening . . . soft breezes (he gets into position, one hand on his thigh, the other raised to the sky). Here we go . . . (after a moment his face clouds over with the look of a man who has just suffered a totally unexpected accident and straightening up he holds himself tightly in) I *have* been taken short . . . goodbye! (He pivots round and goes off running at full speed.)